Copyright © Sandra Bacon. All Rights Reserved

No part of this publication may be reproduced, stored in a retrieval system or transmitted in any way or by any means. This means electronic, mechanical, photocopying, recording or otherwise, without the prior written consent of the author of this publication. Any person or persons who do may be liable to criminal prosecution and civil claims for damages.

Ancient Civilization Mandalas

Animal Mandalas

Alien Mandalas

Art Decco Mandalas

Egyptian Mandalas

Love Mandalas

Sacred Mandalas

Skull Mandalas

Tribal Mandalas

Steampunk Mandalas

www.ingramcontent.com/pod-product-compliance
Lightning Source LLC
Chambersburg PA
CBHW081433220526
45466CB00008B/2374